f

F

poems

FRANZ WRIGHT

Alfred A. Knopf

New York   2013

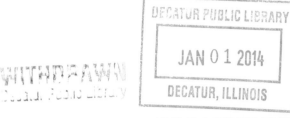

THIS IS A BORZOI BOOK
PUBLISHED BY ALFRED A. KNOPF

Copyright © 2013 by Franz Wright

All rights reserved. Published in the United States by Alfred A. Knopf,
a division of Random House, Inc., New York, and in Canada
by Random House of Canada Limited, Toronto.

www.aaknopf.com/poetry

Knopf, Borzoi Books, and the colophon are registered trademarks of
Random House, Inc.

Library of Congress Cataloging-in-Publication Data
Wright, Franz, [date]
[Poems. Selections]
F : poems / by Franz Wright.—First edition.
pages ; cm.
"This is a Borzoi Book."
ISBN 978-0-307-70158-9
I. Title.
PS3573.R5327F17 2013
811'.54—dc23
2013004588

Jacket design by Carol Devine Carson

Manufactured in the United States of America
First Edition

For Elizabeth, with infinite love
And for our friends Lydia and Cora
forever young

The Hacs have arranged to rear every year a few child martyrs . . . raggedy, wretched, hopeless kids . . . whom they subject to atrocious mistreatment and evident injustices, inventing reasons and deceptive complications based on lies, for everything, in an atmosphere of terror and mystery. In this way they have brought up great artists, poets.

—HENRI MICHAUX, "IN THE LAND OF THE HACS"
(BASED ON RICHARD ELLMANN'S TRANSLATION)

CONTENTS

III

f

FOUR IN THE MORNING

Wind from the stars.
The world is uneasily happy—
everything will be forgotten.

The bird I've never seen
sang its brainless head off;
same voice, same hour, until

I woke and closed my eyes.
There it stood again:
wood's edge, and depression's

deepening
shade inviting me in
saying

No one is here.

No one was there
to be ashamed of me.

I

ELDERLY COUPLE

Those last two weeks of August before we too are married, before we recognize another soul in town, we meet them walking here at evening, nod, and smile hello. Until we don't awhile, then never again. Small rabbits tensely watch us pass from the long uncut grass between headstones where they believe they are safe. They have gone to school with stones to learn patience and motionlessness. Rapidly graying, dissolving into one substance with the dusk, they are so still they tremble. They are troubled by a fear whose source they have no way of comprehending, combined with the equally incomprehensible delight of children playing hide-and-seek as it gets dark, sooner, enormously, with every passing day, and they become aware in waves of being older than a person they were only yesterday. While the trees swaying soundlessly high overhead, the breeze and first visible stars seem, if anything, younger. Mothers stand in yellow kitchen windows pretending to listen to fathers quietly, inconsequentially droning on behind them in the deepening evening, even when they are the voices of men no longer alive. They say things like "Any day above ground is a good day . . ." And what would they have known about that? The mothers stand completely still, they will never turn around. Standing with his back to a tree, barely breathing, a boy wonders if he is going to be the one abruptly struck down from above, swiftly carried aloft over the first soft lights of town by huge wings, never to be seen again, and decides that he probably won't, and for a minute is perfectly happy.

Mt. Feake Cemetery, 1999

THROUGH

Once upon the eternally recurring dark before the dawn, flashing its green neon NO VACANCY sign repeatedly down the unsightseeing one-lane unraveling etcetera highway. Forever. Can Tucson be far behind? Mile-wide highway of crushed emerald polished to an adamantine coolness, noontime and moontime, one unmoving cloud in its depths, continuing straight ahead toward the line where the blue abyss of Arizona falls away (just trying to think positive). Then you suddenly woke at the wheel, took the next exit, stood at my door, and not a moment too soon. I am sick of being chained to this chair and told what to write, much of it outrageous lies! Once, I feel sure of it, when death had no vacancy you came and stayed in me. Or did I come and stay in you, the last word long set down, unfinished? Through.

LEAVE ME HIDDEN

I was having trouble deciding
which to watch: *Night
of the Living Bloggers*, or
Attack of the Neck-Brace People.
In the end I just went for a walk.

In the woods I stopped wondering why
of all trees
this one: my hand
pressed to fissures
and ridges of

bark's hugely magnified
fingerprint, forehead
resting against it
finally, feeling
distinctly

a heartbeat, vast, silently
booming there deep in
my hidden leaves, blessed
motherworld, personal
underworld, thank you

thank you.

I DREAMED I MET
WILLIAM BURROUGHS

I met William Burroughs in a dream.
It was some sort of bohemian farmhouse,
and he was enthroned, small and skeletal,
in a truly gigantic red armchair.

When I asked him how he was, he replied,
Well, you know what they say—for best results
always mock and frighten lobster before boiling.
Franz—I like that name, Franz. Childe Franz

to the dark tower something or other . . . Hey,
got a smoke? And quit worrying so much:
they can't help themselves, they're like abused dogs
and they're going to react to affection and kindness

with uncontrollable savagery. Just tell them,
You're out of my mind, pal. You're out
of my mind. Either that or, I'm out of yours.
That'll keep them brain-chained to their trees.

ROADSIDE GRAVE:
WINTER, MASS

In the white is a name.
In the three worlds
it stands. Wind
sounds, a world of one
color.
Name spoken,
once,
across a darkening field;
name being stitched,
very small, in white thread
in white cloth.

FATALVILLE, ARK

To you this world's the other world. The first transparent leaves wind-blown to spreading green flames—how strange everything looks all at once, my room looks different, and I am afraid of it. You'll never guess why the universe just turned into somebody's name, the morning light a look of love: a single double-nostriled blast (40 mg per). A single white rose glows on the tabletop, filling the room with the distant and close to inaudible voices singing from its whorled earlike depths, the connection nearly lost . . . What can you do but walk toward it? I cross the room for several years staying one step ahead of the avalanche and resisting attempting, at each star-filled canyon's ledge, flight. I reach the bed at last and lie down, like you entertaining no need whatsoever to open my eyes, to move my hand, or pronounce another word, ever. Let someone else give it a try, and they will, too. My friend I never met, I think you would agree: the deans are never going to let that cow go. I don't wonder how many more of them there are these days, all those masters of the art in their early twenties, just like John Keats and Hart Crane! We don't have to think about it anymore. The poet will come, no matter what they do.

HOMECOMING

It took longer than expected to walk to my old elementary school. I can't tell you how long it took. And by the time I got there, I was certain, it would be too late to get inside and have a look around. It was suddenly night and I found myself at the main entrance. Do you think the moon is larger on their coast than ours? It seems that way to me: larger and a good deal more brilliant, I don't know why. It's not something I feel comfortable discussing. But I know that I can talk to you. I have always felt that I could turn to you. The door was unlocked, to my surprise, though every light in the building was off. Blindingly the moon burned into each classroom as it glided by, until I stood outside the door of mine. Finding it slightly ajar I pushed it wide open with one hand, shielding my eyes with the other; heard more than saw a dead leaf skitter across the floor, hopelessly giving away my position. I realized I could not move for the room fallen from its former murmurous to absolute quiet, followed by a unanimous turning of faces in my direction, the humorous and lethal eyes of great leaders gathered in secret all trained on me for a long minute—a minute with seasons—before slowly returning to whatever it is they actually talk about. And I for one am glad they are willing to keep such secrets from us. For us. I don't want to know. I don't want to know anything anymore. All at once they were children sitting around the circular table in formal attire far too large for them, heads bowed, eyes closed as in prayer, then wearily raised and gazing straight through me: twelve brothers and sisters torn from sleep by their mad father who had just been explaining to them why they must all die.

THE COMPOSER

People said he was overly fond of the good life and ate like a pig. Yet the boy who brought him his chocolate in bed would sometimes find him weeping quietly, both plump pink hands raised slightly and conducting, evidently, in small brief genuflective feints. Awareness of existing in a universe where death is real came to him in the form of music.

STAY

The clouds were pretending to be clouds
when in fact they were overheard comments
regarding his recent behavior, but muffled

as though heard through a wall. Unlike
the personal messages being conveyed to him
in the form of asides by people on TV, chilling

in their calm and unequivocal malevolence.
In the garden the roses were opening,
chanting in unison, My name is Mary and

you really don't want to come near me,
not if I was the last little swastika nympho
on earth, and what was that supposed to mean!

Then there were the others who lived there.
(Was he living there now?) They were indifferent
to him with the very striking exception of

two friends. He could tell they were friends
by the marked improvement in their mood
when his was at its most truly desolate.

FOUR SEMI-DREAMT POEMS

1

I am gimp, I am misspell.

I am *Kind,*
I am
kränkliches Lächeln.

Don't touch me,
I am
drown.

Am room of
never
leave.

2

Rodent doll
we are beginning
to affix the black petals
to your feet
and hands
now and then
it will be up to you
to nimbus your own small
skull gnawed down

to crew cut
and filled
with silver
human hair.

3

Caducean
their limbs
entwining
wielded
though
by what
and to what
purpose neither
knew. Name me
someone who
knew.

4

Day before the last snow;
a one-legged pigeon
lights on the bench,
sidles over and looks
right into my eyes.

In the empty park,
waiting alertly
for X,
who doesn't show.

WHISPERED CEREMONY

Like a kneeling communicant offering his candle the white scorpion has lifted its lance and touched the right spot. It is only through the most vigilant patience and resignation, the readiness, in fact, to die in wait without the vaguest idea of why you are there, what it is you are supposed to accomplish, or the greater purpose of this action, that you may hope to master the unparaphrasable and lightninglike agility that allows it to strike, strike and withdraw and be gone in the same instant. One day the accumulated force of its current and all the tensions coiled within it will burst, flood, and sweep from the planet the final sinister utopia. Narcissus, goldenly unbuttoning themselves in the field's heart. The king of the alders is dying.

POSTCARD 2

Incomprehensible fate that sentenced my mother and father, steadfast and devoted friends once, to marriage. I can't say I blame him, I would have left the raving bitch myself, and would do so many many times in years to come.

Then, of course, I came along. And there is a limit to what one man may endure. So, I suppose I am the reason he left home. I am the one to blame. He did his best, he gave what he had. It was shit, it was words stretched three thousand miles, but it was all he had, his hushed mite, and he gave it gladly, writing once a year like clockwork. He rarely remembered to mail what he'd written, poor man, when I think of what I must have put him through: barely legible one-sentence postcards he sometimes worked at half the night. But as they all said the same thing, word for word, missing out on a year, two or three in a row sometimes, wasn't so bad. He should be forgiven. *The blizzard I visit your city disguised as will never arrive and never be over . . .* I think what he was trying to say was that at some point I'd begin to notice I was freezing, wasn't dressed right, had nowhere to go, and was staggering into a blinding storm that no one else could see. I think he meant, *The cold will make you what I am today.*

LAMP

Evening street of midnight blue with here and there a lighted window. Of the at home, or the possibly not. Concentrically into the air whose blue sphere gradually gives way to pure lethal space, wave after wave of a pale cadmium yellow expanding into emptiness and past the blood-brain barrier. Lamp manufactured unwittingly in the image of its maker the mind, which goes on emitting dim rays from its frail bulb of skull, from its insignificant and evidently random sector of an infinite place all its own; mind illuminating not much: seen, say, from its own frozen and excommunicated Pluto, it is nearly indistinguishable from any other. All minds are pretty much the same, they'll tell you so themselves, but secretly each is devoted to the conviction that it is irreparably different from all the rest—in fact, it is this in which they are most fundamentally alike.

ONE

Bodies are endless but sentience
gazing from endlessly various eyes
is one, and I can prove it.

Music's an idealized and
disembodied nervous system.
Who's the sacrificial famous person now?

The angel of death is the angel of birth.
Look, look, the monster
has tears in his eyes.

A pair of dark glasses
smoking a cigarette;
a pair of dark glasses initially

and solely manufactured
for use by ancient
Chinese judges.

When you die the world
is going to die, the world
and all the stars—

what dies when you are born?

When you have to take it to feel, more
or less, the way you once felt
when you weren't taking it,

I'll meet you at high moon.

I'll greet you
there, the other
last speaker of a language.

At the trial of sleep,

theoretically, I will be seeing you.
In the aisles of the pharmacy
open all night, I'll be waiting. Outside

the locked glass door to the insane
asylum dollhouse childhoods
like yours, I'll keep vigil;

at the marriage of never happen
and eternity, I will be you.
At the velvet heart-shaped dark

green morning glory leaves,
dragonfly, sister, and bride
by unbreakable vow

of *not-here-return-*
to-sender
silence, please.

CRUMPLED-UP NOTE
BLOWING AWAY

Were no one
here to witness it,
could the sun be
said to shine? Clearly,
you pedantic fool.

But I've said all that
I had to say.
In writing.
I signed my name.
It's death's move.

It can have mine, too.
It's a perfect June morning,
and I just turned eighteen;
I can't even believe
what I feel like today.

Here am I, Lord,
sitting on a suitcase,
waiting for my train.
The sun is shining.
I'm never coming back.

II

What does midnight have to say?

—NIETZSCHE

ENTRIES OF THE CELL

Tell me once more how you're going to do it. I have been wondering and
wondering. Tell me. By windowlight, my ghosts; by winterlight,
sun seen from Pluto, handmirror of dead girl and ground-
diamond desert; by taste of fresh bird blood in snow, theorem
and spell. By muttering and crooning alone the same word I've
been saying to reach you, forever it seems, from glad ascent to
fatal fall, and all I have seasick and brainsick been trying to
recall, dying to sing you, be it ever so simple and strange.

There are two infinities. Can't you see them?

Don't ask me how it works—one of star-sown space, and one of
the words for it—. . .

I only know it was like living twice.

Rilke said even in prison you would have your childhood,
incontrovertible proof he had never been anywhere near a prison.

He also said death begins at the tip of the nose, now that's interesting!
And I am still riding the trains amassing corroboratory examples.

But I know something nobody taught me and I never learned
in a book.

They aren't evil.

They aren't even evil. They're just a disease, or its infinitesimal wings.

Not a fatal disease. Not necessarily.

Without premeditation, mindlessly, without discrimination they
communicate themselves to anyone who comes within their
range . . .

I have suffered from them and I know.

And I have been them.

Then I saw the freeways encircling Los Angeles strangled with white
hearses, bumper to bumper, moving along about 10 mph . . .

Headlights in daylight following one after another, mysterious
commonplace: who has never stopped to let them pass
without an elongated second of identification with the absent
person riding; without a pang of sick panic,

or one of envy?

I like to light a candle after Mass, stare into the flame brimming
     with one honey-colored tear, and ask that today You visit the
     heart of someone in need of You, someone who's left the door
     open although he does not believe You would heal him, does not
     believe You are on the way, not today, not yesterday, not ever. Visit
     especially somebody who cannot believe in your existence and
     must be as lonely as You are. I see You raised up a few feet off the
     ground, face no longer clenched in pain, crucified cadaver, thin
     arms still outstretched to draw all to You, and *why can't I respond?*
     Even now, after ten years of more or less failing to act like a
     believer, no more capable of maintaining a literal sense of Your
     presence than I am of staring directly into the sun—even now
     You have not forsaken me.

For all intents and purposes abandoned, Your love unrequited, You have
     not turned away from my mind, its former numb and sleepless
     coma. And I know my failure to perceive You can in no way
     diminish the fact that You are here!

I light my candle, I stand a minute looking down at it, and ask.

Dusk-colored mountain and mountain of dusk looming starrily,
     peakless, behind it—at the mountain of *How* I am kneeling, the
     mountain of *Why, why?*

There is a step to take beyond the final step.

Mr. Wright? May we ask to speak with you?

Sir, looking back on a long and illustrious career in diplomacy and as a
      man admired the world over as much for your patience, calm, and
      tact under the most stressful of circumstances as your devotion
      to the dignity of friend and enemy alike, we wonder whether you
      would care to comment on a subject which has become, in recent
      months, the source of unusually intense, even embittered debate
      in nearly every major walk of life, from business to business on
      the one hand, to business, business, and business on the other.
      Sir, is it your opinion that the world, beneath its tumultuous
      and often incomprehensible surface, is a vale in which souls are
      individually, painstakingly crafted one by one, as has generally
      been held for some centuries, or do you find yourself siding with
      the radical but increasingly popular view of it as their slippery,
      gory, and unspeakable slaughterhouse . . .

Strangers my family became, complete stranger who became my family!

I will die with a hammer in my hand, says the glass anvil.

And were your feelings so terrible and dark they could not be turned
    into fuel?

Refused their leaden drugs. I left and walked home, walked through walls,
    crossed the river and sat in a room for ten years and worked.
    For I left that gigantic locked windowless place hidden away in
    plain sight. Building without an address where the speechless and
    screaming

That's right, I had left the vast bed I'd been sharing with madness's other
    most frequent fliers; left them snoring in blank black Risperidal
    slumber, and through one locked ward after another I passed, a
    breeze a sixteenth of an inch from the floor under each of the
    triple-locked doors. Goodbye metal mirror I passed out at crack
    of doom, at (gentian) dawn, and I was gone. I must have died
    all at once, near the end of a sad dream of home; or one that
    featured crushing and irreversible shame.

One bringing to mind's eyes the sentient rays, beloved eyes
    remembered, voices remembered. Or one of strange brothers
    reunited at last. On a bookshelf. Maybe one all about how to tell,
    when you look back, your being lifted up from the mirthful and
    hooted derision that is going to accompany your best days.

Maybe one of the love that was going to give back all the
    time lost for its sake. Of

the planet so alone in timeless night . . .

I walked the length of Boston, still the morning had
    not come.

And where was everyone?

Polaris no longer the North Star.

Where is the bridge that connects the unnameable name and the word
    without world? Which is the bride which the bird? What shining
    is being spanned so far below anyway—that can't be water . . .

Cross of Hiroshima

ash traced on a forehead.

The black dove sent out and still out there.

I'm lying facedown in bed, both arms outstretched, coming in low with my
        lights out.

It can't be long now, and I'm really looking forward to inheriting the
        world I have heard so much about!

Strictly speaking, I haven't heard anything; but I have dreamed of it so
        much.

And what an honor, to be born on earth and take my place among
        the gentle and good, the peace-loving, joyous and free, not to
        mention the compassionate, enlightened, incandescently selfless
        and wise . . .

I think it's a bed. I'm not really that sure where I am, some sort of
        rooming house or lower depths rehab. I've been here for a while,
        and it is my painful duty to report, if anyone's still listening, our
        mission has run into some serious turbulence, to put it mildly.

The glaringly self-evident fact is we are only here today due to direct
    descent from the cruelest, the least burdened by empathy, the
    most covetous, greedy, and sleeplessly obsessed with dominance
    and its maintenance and therefore, as well, the most paranoid,
    puritanical, preemptively savage and hellbent on being the last
    left standing.

My idea is the law should obey us, orphan boy tobacco . . .

We find no evidence of those others. The more generous, utopian and
    inward-looking others who would not have been doing a lot of
    procreating past a certain point.

We have so far managed, by dint of the most arduously disciplined
    deceit, to blend in and give away none of the abhorrence with
    which we naturally contemplate the state of things here.

The honest truth, we've also thrown a couple pretty wild parties, thanks.

This has been an extremely interesting experience, and I am sure it has
    given us all a lot to think about.

Right at the moment I am sitting at a very small desk beside a small
    child who can't write, doesn't draw or play much, and has never
    said a single word to anyone as far as I know.

A flawlessly beautiful child with perfect white sharp tiny teeth, long
    straight blonde hair, and profoundly intelligent dark blue sad eyes.
    A perfectly lovely little girl who has no name, and is one hundred
    thousand years old.

The cell will teach you all things.

There are spots in the sea, depths where light ceases to penetrate,
    a painless, dreamless and shatterproof sleep holy to horrible
    workers: the ones who'll appear in our place after we've fallen
    storming the walls of the Kingdom.

If I tell you her breasts are two small blind pink dolphins who live
    unmolested, in eternal delight, in some unnamed river of South
    America, what are you going to do about it?

And what's it about, all the dissension over God.

    The word *God*.

The word tree has put no leaf out yet.

We were born, we supposed, knowing everything. All the most
    important words addressed to us went in one ear and
    encountering minimal resistance right out the other, but

look who was doing the addressing.

The investigations were always being led by those who'd most brilliantly
    and deniably benefited from the crime.

Northern Ohio, September '74. Nixon murders Allende.

Violet light of the wheat, we were growing old and dying young.

How much did we drink, how often, and why?

We drank.

When it rains, you don't ask how many raindrops fell. You say it rained.

Lots of rain, many semicolons— . . . the cell will teach you all.

This blue world.

Unattainable—stranger than dying,

by what, what unmerited blessing, were we allowed to come here
and to see it, as in a dream, or with eyes of flesh, what difference?

Death row born and bred, and yet

This blue world,

my stranger . . .

Anticipate at least a year of total unresponsive silence.

Include a stabbed self-undressed envelope, if you ever hope to see your
sorry work again.

There were a couple decades when this was my primary—no, my sole
concern.

Anguish, grieving: you will get over them. That's the problem.

Even this is taken from you, in the end there is nothing that will not be
taken, this last connection with someone, your good hand like a
bridge already burning when you get there.

In an old notebook I have come across a dream entry from September:
an airliner's parked, engines coming on while all the windows
remain dark, in the middle of a baseball field a few blocks away.

And look what I've come across in the middle of these disintegrating
pages.

It's a capital *F* that takes up a whole page.

My name, or grade in life?

In color a dull dead rust-red, someone's blood, and I can't
imagine whose.

But never mind about that—let's take a good look at this *F.*
Think about it and tell me,

who names their child Franz and throws him to the boys of
        American grade schools?

Franz. It would make a good name for a dog. Some retired
        shepherd, perhaps

the great-great-great-great-great-great-grandson of one whose
        job was herding naked people.

He's out of work now, our friend Franz.

He's had his assignments, an occasional elderly blind man
        here, a stint on the trains there,

helping silent uniformed men hunt down ticket delinquents;

he has been seen slinking in and out of certain still-bombed-out
        churches, limping along behind the pack, serving as some
        cowering junkie's skinny and worried-looking defender,

in the German light. I think. There have been so many wars, even since
        that last major mass murder/suicide, I can't keep them straight.
        So many psychotically futile traveling killing floors for the
        amusement of a few delusional and limitlessly powerful flabby
        old family men.

Meanwhile, here on the other side, wandering the streets, our Franz is
    abruptly bashed in the shoulder by some very large oncoming
    passerby. "Sorry," he mutters in his sleep, as he goes by. And
    "How's it going."

An individual I do not know, like pretty close to everyone on earth.

And like close to everyone on earth he does not actually give a shit
    about how, for me, it happens to be going.

But it's an interesting question.

The truth is I'm not feeling so good;

and to judge from their expressions neither is anyone else.

Not as bad, say, as the pregnant girl who's just been diagnosed with an
    inoperable malignancy, missed her train by seconds, and stands
    there on the platform in the hot stench of its wake.

Nearby the witnessing angel who shows up at all such events, white
    glare where the face is supposed to be, unseeable for its
    brightness.

And how hideous he is, we would think, could we see him.

We who unreflectingly gaze every day of our lives into the perfectly
     bland face of evil, smiling back at us though strictly avoiding
     physical contact—it is all recorded; as literally everything else
     is, in any room of company or solitude on earth, any encounter
     between two or more human beings is captured in a still frame
     stored away, a timeless tableau behind glass in one of the secret
     museums . . .

So far from home, messenger who has long forgotten the message . . .

Face monstrous with thirteen million years of looking on
     and grieving,

grieving for the languageless mother keeping her distance
     and watching intently as a large doglike
     creature is eating her child, for instance;

mourning the small girl with the missing bird, vacant cage
     clutched to her chest, calling out its name,
     parents lost in the crowd, unmarked train
     cars slowing.

The other day while reading I came across the long-deceased
expression "You are the love of my life."
I did not sneer, or bare my teeth in derision.
I stopped a moment, leaned down, put my ear
to it and listened, hard, because who knows
what might not still be beating or breathing in
there—some vividly literal meaning like You
personify to me the love of life . . .

Then I remembered how long long ago I had bought it, the
whole illusion, everything from the most
remote star to the bubble of time that will burst
before I can finish this phrase; everything from
the small bloody scream of our first appearance
to our speechless and forsaken exit. All will be
forgotten, everything you perceived, thought,
dreamed, hoped, remembered . . . all the past
all the crawling fucking coughing chestpounding
nose-picking and deathward attempts
to make real some desperate desire, like
standing upright for a minute in the sun. The
sun that will die.

First walker, seafarer, spacefarer—where did it start,
　　how, and why? Show me the first to form
　　words, the first to weep, the first to sing. The
　　first to kill not others but himself. The first to
　　die for someone else.

A member of our species wrote Love, which moves the sun
　　and other stars, and saw it animating all that is.

And the darkness has neither overwhelmed nor comprehended it,
　　yet.

Love. Of all things least illusory.

Love which whispers *It is so simple: what you need, provide.*

Let's say that five a.m. arrives and finds you fully dressed in
　　yesterday's clothes,

the clock set for six.

It's bad, no question about it, and yet.

What a relief it will be, won't it—stumbling out once more
        to see the morning street with its familiar
        million strangers streaming past, you standing
        there watching them part with blind eyes
        around you on either side, God bless them,
        every one, everyone who's not going to hurt
        you today, all the strangers, how you love
        them all at once, how close you feel to them.

Because the soul is a stranger in this world.

III

DEDICATION

It's true I never write, but I would gladly die with you.
Gladly lower myself down alone with you into the enormous mouth
that waits, beyond youth, beyond every instance of ecstasy,
        remember?
Before battle we would do each other's makeup, comb each other's
        hair out,
saying we are invincible, we are terrible and splendid—
the mouth waiting, patiently waiting. And I would meet you there
        again
beyond bleeding thorns, the endless dilation, the fire that alters nothing;
I am there already past snowy clouds, balding moss, dim
swarm of stars even we can step over, it is easier this time, I
        promise—
I am already waiting in your personal Heaven, here is my hand,
I will help you across. I'd gladly die with you
right now, although I cannot
seem to write
from this gray institution. See
we are so busy trying to cure me;
and I'm condemned—sorry, I have been given the job
of vacuuming the desert forever, well, no less than eight hours
        a day.
And it's really just about a thousand miles of cafeteria;
a large one in any event. With its miniature plastic knives,
its tuna salad and saran-wrapped genitalia will somebody
        please

get me out of here, sorry. I am happy to say that
every method, massive pharmaceuticals, art therapy
and edifying films as well as others I would prefer
not to mention—I mean, every single technique
known to the mouth—sorry!—to our most kindly
compassionate science is being employed
to restore me to normal well-being
and cheerful stability. I go on vacuuming,
toward a small diamond light burning
off in the distance. Remember
me. Do you
remember me?
In the night's windowless darkness
when I am lying cold and numb
and no one's fiddling with the lock, or
shining flashlights in my eyes,
although I never write, deep down
I long to die with you,
does that count?

LEARNING TO READ

If I had to look up every fifth or sixth word
so what. I looked them up.
I had nowhere important to be.

My father was unavailable, and my mother
looked like she was about to break,
and not into blossom, each time I spoke.

My favorite was *The Iliad*. True,
I had trouble pronouncing the names;
but when was I going to pronounce them, and

to whom?
My stepfather maybe?
Number one, he could barely speak English—

two, he had sufficient cause
to smirk or attack
without prompting from me.

Loneliness boredom and fear
my motivation
fiercely fueled.

I get down on my knees and thank God for them.

Du Fu, the Psalms, Whitman, Rilke.
Life has taught me
to understand books.

PANHANDLER

He's manning his spot on the sidewalk, as always, though I've been gone so long. Just inside the doorway he appears to have exclusive rights to. He stands so still he might be an old crane on the banks of a narrow gray river at dusk. He might be a headstone that never got a name, or guardian of the boundary between us and a country where our doubles go about our day, identical to the second, but with quiet, tact, calm, and unfailing kindness. We're a planet of cold-blooded fuckers, but somehow he managed to outfucker us all: here he is, still on his feet, shoulders straight, sort of, right upper arm more or less perpendicular to the pavement, and extended parallel to that pavement the forearm ending at the skinny necklike wrist protruding from its baggy and too-short shirt cuff with the open hand held out palm upward as though he were offering to sell you its emptiness, or patiently waiting for the toll.

ROSE OPENING

1

The soundless glacial splintering of the first glass knell would spell its last, attracting as it had a squadron of black attack dragonflies.

2

The soundless splintering of the first glass knell would appear to have coincided, in fact become one with its last, having fatefully announced its presence to a nearby flock of tiny but remarkably ravenous moon-colored piranha moths, known to reach sizes so small as to render them literally invisible, sometimes even when examined under powerful instruments of magnification.

3

The rose opened. It took quite a long time, in our terms. Strange, incidentally, how magically advanced our terms are when you consider how comically inept their creators, how grotesquely, lethally stupid and blind. I am, of course, speaking figuratively. To insinuate the vaguest defamation of the blind is in no way my intent, I want to make this crystal clear, a still small knell through the whorls of your ear; because if I have, all my life, identified with any group of human beings at all it would have to be the blind. Nevertheless, it must be admitted that the hallmark, birthmark, and tattooed number of your typical human is a severe disability when it comes to concerning themselves with or even perceiving anything beyond the most immediate consequences of their every action, word, or favorite sleeping position. Don't ask me, but I have always been mystified by the taste of the word itself. Blind. I like to say it—why would that be? I love it when it is pronounced by Christ: you feel a child could grasp that he is saying something more than what he's saying. The rose opened. Rose. This word, it too leaves nothing else to say. What if we just allow it to be a rose—not miraculous enough for you? As the heart. But that's another story, the heart, with its neverending haunted longings for everything but what it has. There are indomitable hearts that take the pain and will not die, and I suppose there are shriveled remnants of that organ wandering around, there are, I have been of them, and somehow returned, and I have good news. The rose opened. The literal rose. And its word. The word thinks it is the object it stands for, but leave it alone, let the word be a place, for those who could not find one here. And sometimes there are no words. There are none for what happens when you breathe in the rose there are no words for, and so what—does there have to be a word for everything! Take this abandoned bird's nest. You can talk about it for a moment and take it deep into yourself, you know a fraying gray abandoned bird's nest is not a fraying gray abandoned bird's nest. Love the one inside you who is not articulate or smart, who's hardly spoken all her life, and in this way spared something for herself. Get to know her, she can teach you so much, and rest yourself. Will you do that for me? Learn to go deaf, mute, and unlearned as heaven come hiddenly into you. Pay everyone, let them fight over your wallet, let them tear it to pieces like dogs. Then, in the first evening waves, walk to your lake, leave your body and go for a long swim. More wisdom from the elders: if you see it, please pluck the slightest shoot of the inane myth of hell, dreamed up and ratified long, long ago by important self-haters of the past and viciously maintained by others like them right down to this day. Do exactly what the rose inside your chest is telling you to do; go without food if you have to occasionally—I never died of it, I think it was good for me. Accept the jeering lashes of the imbecilic world, seek the human in its singularity, the one alone, who is good, who is hurt, who like you still holds on to a hope. Don't let the wrong person know you are happy! Keep it alight, the frail rose in the mind. Remember that there is a nakedness under your nakedness no one can reach. And nakednesses under nakednesses, petals of the rose around you I will one day have the eyes to see. (Don't worry, I won't be watching you ALL the time! I'm not going to stare at you all the time!) And talk to me a little, a traveler just like I was. Say you're having trouble staying awake sometime—pull over right away, put your head back. Give yourself some rest, God bless you. Close your eyes, and tell me what you see.

MEDICINE CABINET

It seemed to take half the day to reach the bathroom, lugging my head in the crook of my arm like a bowling ball containing a hundred pounds of cotton, also dragging it behind me like unto a kite of lead, then, like a flaccid balloon, or the pink misshapen features of a child born with no brain, and I'll tell you, I was about a quarter to dead. That little twinge I'd started out with? Off the smiley/frowny pain chart, children, my garden of scars. Now my whole body felt as if someone had been going at it with a baseball bat as I struggled to awaken this morning long ago. From having mastered and, I have this great fear, memorized the new manual of gender-correct English usage and just good old plain personal experience I can tell you the avoidance of mirrors represents one of humankind's major ordeals among the stars, and I approached this medicine cabinet determined that there should be no eye contact, no full frontal glimpse of myself whatsoever. I knew that I looked like death getting ready to eat a cracker! Were you aware, incidentally, that heroin was invented by Bayer, the familiar aspirin company (thanks, Friedrich)? Or that it remained, in liquid form, an effective over-the-counter cough suppressant until its disappearance from the shelves of American pharmacies in 1910? One day I am going to start to cry and never stop until I die. So what. An hour later I could still be found there gnawing my way through the first gray pill, which was about the size of a pie and must have weighed ten pounds.

SPELL

Some fish for words from shore while others, lacking in such contemplative tact, like to go wading in up to their chins through a torrent of bone-chilling diamond, knife raised, to freeze-frame incarnadine then bid it with hermetic wand flow on, ferociously, transparently, name writ in river.

HOME SOUGHT

For 1 hypodermic syringe with small wings, the ones preferred by the god in his sky-blue hightops. Never used, needless to say. (Well, maybe once at the very most.) Enjoys darting from one shadowy spot in the room to another (or was that only in my X-rays), with the glittering, transitionless movements of hummingbirds or electrons. I seem to have lost it— temporarily!—and I am afraid, harshly attributing this new symptom to pre-traumatic stress disorder. Actually, that was the name of a dance craze in the early nineteen fifties. See what I mean? Nobody remembers the good things. It's just textbook chronic momentary insanity. When did we become so competitive with our diagnoses? And all the while the poor thing is hovering right above my head, like the cartoon representation of thought. Strangely has made no attempt at escape, even though I am standing in front of the high open windows where I can so often be found. Earthly blue and heaven bound. The rest of the time I'm in bed having this black-and-white dream about standing in front of a window, a high open window. All right, now I see it, very clearly embubbled above my skull—a great notion on the part of my surviving brother, double and handicapped shadow, one leg an inch short, the limping starless wing of my own flesh and the ideas he entertains in a bright dream, and one I have entertained so long, brightly. It appears we are having the same dream, in shifts, unpublishable to this day.

RECURRING AWAKENING

So I stop a tall girl all in blue on the hall
and receive first a harried and desultory apology
then, point-blank, news that you passed late last night.
You passed at three-thirty in the morning.
What was it, some sort of exam?
She smiles at herself,
epicenter of this
revelation, I find myself walking along
a high ridge in the wake of an ice storm
at the heart of some annihilated fairy tale
of forest in West Virginia,
redwing blackbirds'
feet clenched to one crystal branch
per deceased tree: eyes stitched shut
and beaks wide open.
And finally, there it is: your face, floating
at my feet with nose pressed to transparent black ice;
yes, you are certainly dead, all the signs point to it.
Wrapped in white cerements,
white face more youthful
and grave than I have ever seen it, frowning slightly
as though it were reading, one eye blind
in a blonde swath of hair,
vague smile like the velvet depression
the lost diamond has left in its case;
now strangely you are moving

in a wide circle around me, stepping
sideways in time
to some slow stately dance
hand in hand
with the handless
in their identical absence
of affect, lips moving in unison.
I can't hear a thing, but it's said
the instant of being aware that we are sleeping
and the instant of waking are one
and the same—and thus, against delusion
we possess this defense.
Only if you refuse
to respond, if I can only write you,
and write on black wind-blurred water, what's the use?

TO

Before you were I loved you
and when you were born
and when you took your first step
Although I did not know
good luck I want to whisper

lone penguin keep sturdily waddling
in the direction of those frozen
    mountains sister
of desolate sanctity
I want to scream
Although I did not know

I loved you later on
as just a weedy thing
a little skeleton I loved
Both long pre-you a child myself
and as a man in retrospect

I loved and I was there
while they were raping you
I loved although
like God
that's all I could do.

DAWN MOON OVER CALVARY

Limestone fragment of an angel, its lips half healed over with someone's half-legible name, one whose watch stopped dead decades ago. The moon still so bright at four in the morning it casts a distinct sundial-like shadow, nightwind brightwind, right wing a stump; limestone angel from 1915, greenly leprous with the lichen that's covered your throat and has now started in on one cheek. Vacant sockets welling up day by day to darkness with the moon. And adhering to the wall inside the small cave on the left, the ancient arachnid remains of a dust-covered egg sac . . . Young face forever gazing with a look of utmost sweetness skyward; thin fingers clasped, a couple missing, like front teeth, beneath the place in the air that was once your delicate chin. The prostitute who loved Jesus so much, and the woman ashamed in the act of adultery, and the girl whose brother he had brought back from the dead, and the stranger to whom he had spoken at the well, the one who had not heard of him, unable to lower her eyes in his presence, so startled had she been to hear a male stranger's voice addressing her personally, asking if she would not like a drink from the water that would quench her thirst forever: so lonely and desolate had they been in the first days of the life they would have to live without him; what a relief it was to find each other at the place of his tomb, just as it was beginning to get light out. Though immediately they saw that the stone had been moved from in front of the tomb, and that the space inside was empty, his shroud as though della Francesca's victory flag neatly folded upon the stone bed. One of them, after the others had fled, remained at the mouth of the tomb weeping. All the while Jesus, unnoticed, or mistaken for the gardener, had been waiting for her, and without looking up he asked why she was crying. Only yesterday, she replied, the Teacher's body was laid in this place. But now the stone has been moved and the body is not there. Sir, please tell me where they have taken it? He stood and almost turning toward her, hiding his face in the newly risen shadow of an unnamed constellation, his teeth and part of his lower jaw gone, said to her, Mary? Have you come here to mourn for the living? England, 1939. Freud as an alien, an old man with a bandaged face in extreme and constant pain ("quite unnecessary") after one more attempt at a prosthetic jaw, hands Virginia Woolf a lily. Now she is a drowned woman. She believed Germans were on their way, that they had a list of people they intended to murder, and that she was on it. They were; and they did; and she was. But did she have to do it for them? "Mental illness," he wrote somewhere: "a metaphor, one in which the body stands for the soul." Who's off again somewhere no doubt floating face down down a black reverie.

SCREAMED LULLABY

I am more concerned, to tell you the truth, with the eternity that preceded my birth than its famous counterpart in whose presence I will soon be basking, or so I have been told. You know the one, lying directly ahead, no matter which way you turn, no matter how cunning the route, or how agile the evasive maneuver. I don't have time to think about it. I work insane hours and have to be prepared at a moment's notice to perform operations of such fantastic complexity and delicacy, the slightest error, the smallest slipup, may have catastrophic consequences, under conditions so primitive—take the lighting: you'd be hard-pressed to thread a needle in here. We can give the matter our full attention when we have a couple consecutive free decades. Even after all this time, I am amazed, amazed and appalled, by the way the one manifestation of timelessness is constantly in eclipse to the other. In the mind. The one nobody ever forgets about. Death, they call it, and so do I. But does this mean we were dead before we were born? Ah, such thoughts assail me, I am drawn to mental deserts, I am drawn to the genre of speechlessness. A story for another day. The time has come to face the fact that we are in serious arrears with respect to attention paid the first eternity, and must consider the immediate reinstatement of a decent and time-honored attitude of distant but respectful openness to dialogue, if not a posture of outright submission, awe, and fear. To think how often I myself must have contributed, unknowingly, to the avalanche, the silence, the innocent ignorance which is surely the shadow of one more terrible, something I am not going to talk about anymore, I can't. Don't make me. For the time has come to act, or at least make a to-do list. My idea is we ought to approach eternity number 1, offer it a helping hand, who knows, it may be lying hurt somewhere, like the child who disappeared in a tornado years ago, like a defeated and alien king traveling by night, always afraid. It has had so little contact with us—we must come to its aid, but gently, gently though unbidden, we don't want to help it live by scaring it to death. You know what they say: how different the sunlight will look when there's no one to look at it. But never mind all that. There's got to be a way. You and I, for example, could leave the house right this minute and find someplace to light a candle in its name, the first, the mother eternity. Nothing radical's going to be necessary, a hug, choice of story or song, a back rub maybe—these are avenues worth blindly crawling down. I myself am prepared to sit with it for half an hour or so, several times a week if need be. We have taken too little care of this. Think how disappointing, how devastating it would be, as though you'd been born an identical twin but one practically deaf and bald and, oddly, a full half-inch shorter than its golden overshadowing double; a loser, let's face it, with nothing to do day in and day out but watch television, master lip-reading, and brood. It never asked to be born at all. It had not been its plan to grow up the handicapped other, the limping, starless wing of its own flesh.

PEACH TREE

Winds are blessing one by one the unlighted buds of the backbent peach tree's unnoted return. At first light, gray, I stand beside the tree my height: such fragile limbs, as of bark-covered glass—how did we ever survive, find our way back and take again our alien stand here, reappearing at the tip of one of endless branching roads, a dead-end finally? Home. One of quiet's addresses. Where I would endure gratefully five more years, lying low; survive until I couldn't. I had often wondered where it would find me. So, one more northern spring has been given me, too, frail peach tree. You look good. You look like you could go on doing that forever. I have no more idea what I look like than you do, I'm happy to say; all of that is over, that business with the mirror. One winter afternoon I noticed it had stopped. I couldn't anymore, and that was all, wish I'd thought of it sooner. Trembling with the effort not to break, between thumb and forefinger, this one hidden branch I identify with and am trying to lift and lower my eye to. Leaves receding as I reach out, some force in me pushing them away, maybe; I hope that isn't so. Because I want to touch, polishing frictionlessly, the rows of velvet greenest dark beginnings, infolded, growths destined to develop into nothing more than stunted fruit stripped from their boughs overnight by black birds. I wish I could go inside one of them, past the tough rind into one of identical pink erect closed eyelid-colored buds, curl up the size of a comma, and wait there for the softly sifting wind to find me, lift me; wait there alone with everyone else in the darkness before we were born. How did we ever drift into this chill state? I'm feeling kind of bent in half myself; and I see us both bound for the fire, lone peach tree, then nothing, then pure spirit again, even Lazarus has to die—what have I done, what have I been so afraid of all my life?

THE PARTY AT THE END

How many people there were at the party. It was like a small city, I don't think I saw a single person I knew. One remarkable quality of this party was you were allowed to smoke. But you had to sit by yourself on a high stool in a distant corner of the room, facing the wall, and creating an immediately recognizable and oddly unremarked-upon spectacle reminiscent of a punishment for classroom misbehavior minus the tall pointy hat that identified you in certain circles as a wizard and in others as some form of idiot. This odious predicament, while outwardly harmless, was supposed to produce in adventurous but foolhardy boys—it was always a boy, naturally, perhaps one who had been discovered committing some frivolous infraction such as smoking, why not—feelings of terrible shame and remorse, and often figured in humorous movies my friends and I watched after school—there were friends, strangely enough, I am sure of it—movies made during the remote and tumultuous decades preceding our birth, probably to take people's minds off the sad events of the era like the Great Depression and the Second World War. A sense of humor is important and is a character trait, we were led to assume, sadly lacking in the adversary whose scientists, as we now know, had already made the connection between smoking tobacco and a variety of serious, even fatal health problems. The interests of great American enterprise, and its mysterious but essential connection to the liberties we of all the world enjoyed so much, were at stake. So it was of deep and primal necessity, or so these entertainments seemed to suggest, that one remain in high spirits, giving at all times the impression of a winner, with no room in his psyche for vulnerability or fears of defeat and, to prove it, capable of a healthy ability to poke fun at itself, as illustrated in these quaint, archaic films, unavailable to our cruel, brutal and now severely chastised enemies everywhere, whose unspoken message so often involved the danger of embarrassment in matters of criminal rehabilitation while preventing their viewer from thinking very deeply about the issues which led to its necessity in the first place. I hope you are not having trouble following this, I am fairly sure I know what I mean. Those of us still hanging on by our fingernails to social and moral superiority, in the manner of our European ancestors, have always been big on public humiliation; and I suppose the first white people to occupy the land, followed by the not-so-distant founders of what would become this shining republic, this light of opportunity and personal liberty in a world so long darkly deprived of them, found the transplantation of a custom so deeply rooted in their culture, their very sense of reality, easy enough to accomplish. It continued to flourish and combine, in its uniquely fascinating and edifying manner, the upholding of justice with a marvelous source of distraction from personal woes. But I wonder what they would have thought, had they been offered somehow a glimpse into our times, when we have gradually discovered that the same effect may be achieved in a far simpler manner just by ignoring, in a sense denying, the offenders' very existence. And over the past fifteen years (and how much longer it seems!), a new wrinkle has been added to this aspect of the moral code with the appearance of personal computer technology which, like it or not, has now made it possible to publicly humiliate another person, for whatever reason, effortlessly and instantaneously from the comfort of one's home and with near foolproof anonymity. In some cases the taunted have been driven to the very brink—the very brink and over—of madness and/or suicide. This is of course a terribly regrettable and unforeseen side-effect of what most would agree constitutes, at almost every level, a miraculous leap for mankind. It has, of course, tended to erode and even, very rarely, destroy altogether one of the major pillars of justice as we are so fortunate to know it, namely, the right to face your accuser and provide your side of controversial events bound to occur among human beings. But with the exception of a few unstable individuals and those who love and miss them, time passes and heals all. Most accused, in minor matters, simply sit with their face to the wall and gradually, for all intents and purposes, cease to exist for a little while. (It sounds sort of restful.) In our particular case there have been no transgressors, so all's well. And look, I see my old aunt Uglietta, bless her sacred heart, is here and has not left me alone. I don't know what I am doing here in the first place. I loathe my own kind with a loathing entirely beyond the power of words to express, and with equally intense and despairing fervor wish I had never been born. But there she is, thank God. She has made a brief appearance on a couch in the middle of the room, as always compulsively pulling her sleeve down to conceal the livid scars slashed in her left wrist, causing this desolate and solitary woman's fingers to clench partially, inalterably, like a claw—with her too-loud croak of a laugh, and imploring eyes that stare out at you from a face that looks boiled. After a while she lapses into impenetrable silence and smokes incessantly. Everybody tries to pretend she isn't there. After a while, she sighs, turns into cigarette smoke, and is pulled by the silver breeze of late fall afternoon out a window, remaining suspended there a moment like a hanged woman in a gray dress, begins to break up, and is gone.

RAIN IN WALTHAM

Rain in Waltham, the same rain
as anyplace else. So
many minuscule bodies
of dubious water
mixed with dust and risen
from large unknown bodies, then
descending on me
from an all too familiar
sense of foreign sky—same rain
yet different. Don't think I can't tell.
Something about the relentless
and deliberate aim
at the top of my skull.
It's personal. The way it strikes
the window, the way
the woman who lives behind this wall
just took her two hundredth Dilaudid. Or
I finally write you
but can't find an address
anywhere, anywhere—
and I am having trouble dealing
with this most recent illustration
of the impersonal, endlessly patient
indifference of the universe;
and I'm starting to worry again
about this delusional

preoccupation
with a sky that takes sufficient note
of my insignificant anguish
to be indifferent! All my life
I have been asking myself
which is more awful, a sentient
or endlessly unconscious sky?
As if in answer (one
I cannot understand),
all at once my heart is shaken
by a look of love recalled
from twenty years ago. Dan
has just crossed Third Avenue, turning
that fiercely gifted mind on me,
that delighted and cunning
expression which masks
a vast hurt: I won't see it again,
though some days I wonder
if I will ever stop seeing it.
He smiles precisely like an angel. Then
slowly
gives me the finger.
Why did the hospital kill you, Dan?
What had you ever done to it?
I have my own address again.
And if as will sometimes occur,

no matter what you do,
I have to go out
I have a good jacket,
like Larry said you should;
but it's not that much help.
This all started so long ago,
and I am drowning in it now:
the rain of psychosis, the rain
of poverty and love,
the rain in Waltham.

NATIVITY

At the conclusion of nine months'
silent communion,
interrupted on occasion
by long one-sided conversations
of a teary and somewhat excessively candid nature,
and after some very loud mutual screaming,
the two were at last introduced. A shadow
as of vast wings passed across them,
in a manner of speaking: he slept, the
small bud of face unclenched. Later on,
still drowsing, he was relatively certain
he had at some point overheard her claim
that while nursing he never stopped staring
into her eyes, which was fair enough; but
when she added that she felt like she was being judged,
right away he sensed things getting out of hand.
That night he lay awake pondering
the matter for many hours, compelled at last
to find her accusation jejune, massively
unsubstantiated, unwitnessed by anyone
but the accuser, pathetically, and tinged with paranoia—
not a trait, incidentally, you are happy to see
in the person with whom you'll be sharing the next couple decades.
I have done no such thing, he concluded.

In addition, while she remained perfectly free
to fall in line with the mores and laws handed down
by the sheep who exist, his own adamant intent was
to go on waiting for word from his god, who did not.
And, he muttered irritably, "I want a harmonica."

THREE BASHO HAIBUN

I am acquainted with a Kyoto monk by the name of Unchiku who once did a painting. Maybe it was a self-portrait, I don't know. It showed a monk with his face turned away. He asked me if I would write something on it, so I set down these words: You are more than sixty years old, and I am almost fifty. We are both shadows in a dream, the same dream, maybe. Then, as if talking in my sleep, I added my poem:

> *Turn and look back at me*
> *I am so lonely*
> *cold fall night*

2

As the freezing rain of early winter began falling desolately over everything, I sought warmth and company at a roadside inn. Allowed to dry my soaked clothes at the fire, I was further comforted for a time by the innkeeper who tactfully listened to me relate some of the troubles I met with on the road. Suddenly it was evening. I sat down under a lamp, taking great care with them as I produced my ink and brushes, and began to write. Recognizing my work, he solemnly requested that I consider composing a poem in honor of our one brief encounter in this world:

At an inn I am asked for identification
traveler let that be my name
the first winter rain

3

Wherever I travel, wherever I happen to find myself, I am not from there. In fact, the whole world is just such a place to me. I have spent the past six or seven months on the road, a nocturnal traveler who has survived, so far, many devastating illnesses as I made my way onward. I found the more alien I came to seem to myself, the more I missed beloved faces, lifelong friends and aging students, until my steps were drawn irresistibly back toward the outskirts of Edo. And sure enough, day after day they appeared, coming to sit in the small hut of a poor man and talk to me. I had nothing to offer in return except my poem.

I am still alive but why
silvery grass that withers
at the touch of the snow

1690–1692

THE POEM

I am standing alone with everyone else at the center of the world,
a violet ray of noon piercing my forehead.
And all at once it is the middle of the night.

NOTES AND ACKNOWLEDGMENTS

"Roadside Grave: Winter, Mass" was inspired by a line in an early
   poem by Robin Behn.
"The Composer" and "Rain in Waltham" both started as
   translations of, and are now distantly related to, two poems,
   early and late, by Günther Eich.
"Whispered Ceremony" began, about twenty years ago, as a
   relatively literal translation of a brief poem in verse by René
   Char.

Individual poems are dedicated as follows:

"Lamp": Martha McCollough
"Entries of the Cell": Fady Joudah
"Panhandler": Peg Boyers
"Spell": Don Share
"Home Sought": Marshall Wright
"Dawn Moon Over Calvary": Sandra Merrick
"Peach Tree": Deborah Garrison
"Three Basho Haibun": Sam Hamill
"The Poem": Mr. and Mrs. James Haba (This poem is based
   on the famous short poem written by Italian hermeticist
   Salvatore Quasimodo early in the twentieth century.)

Thanks are due to the following publications, where some of the work
in this book first appeared:

Field: "Crumpled-Up Note Blowing Away," "Four in the
 Morning," "Peach Tree"
The New Yorker: "I Dreamed I Met William Burroughs," "Learning
 to Read," "Nativity," "Medicine Cabinet," "Recurring
 Awakening"
Poetry: "Dedication," "Postcard 2," "Spell," "To"
Salmagundi: "Four Semi-Dreamt Poems," "Panhandler,"
 "Through," "Rose Opening"

Some of the work also appeared originally in chapbook form, for
which thanks are due to several presses and their editors: "Entries of the
Cell" (Marrick Press); "Recurring Awakening" (Vallum Chapbook Series).

A NOTE ABOUT THE AUTHOR

FRANZ WRIGHT'S most recent works include *Kindertotenwald* and *Wheeling Motel*. His collection *Walking to Martha's Vineyard* was awarded the Pulitzer Prize in 2004, and he has also been the recipient of two National Endowment for the Arts grants, a Guggenheim Fellowship, and a Whiting Fellowship, among other honors. Wright lives in Waltham, Massachusetts, with his wife, the translator and writer Elizabeth Oehlkers Wright.

A NOTE ON THE TYPE

This book was set in Monotype Dante, a typeface designed by Giovanni Mardersteig (1892–1977). Conceived as a private type for the Officina Bodoni in Verona, Italy, Dante was originally cut only for hand composition by Charles Malin, the famous Parisian punch cutter, between 1946 and 1952. Its first use was in an edition of Boccaccio's *Trattatello in laude di Dante* that appeared in 1954. The Monotype Corporation's version of Dante followed in 1957. Although modeled on the Aldine type used for Pietro Cardinal Bembo's treatise *De Aetna* in 1495, Dante is a thoroughly modern interpretation of the venerable face.

Composed by North Market Street Graphics,
Lancaster, Pennsylvania

Printed and bound by Thomson-Shore,
Dexter, Michigan

Designed by Betty Lew